ALL AROUND THE WORLD
THAILAND

by Kristine Spanier

pogo

Ideas for Parents and Teachers

Pogo Books let children practice reading informational text while introducing them to nonfiction features such as headings, labels, sidebars, maps, and diagrams, as well as a table of contents, glossary, and index.

Carefully leveled text with a strong photo match offers early fluent readers the support they need to succeed.

Before Reading

- "Walk" through the book and point out the various nonfiction features. Ask the student what purpose each feature serves.
- Look at the glossary together. Read and discuss the words.

Read the Book

- Have the child read the book independently.
- Invite him or her to list questions that arise from reading.

After Reading

- Discuss the child's questions. Talk about how he or she might find answers to those questions.
- Prompt the child to think more. Ask: Temples are community gathering places in Thailand. Where does your community come together for special events?

Pogo Books are published by Jump!
5357 Penn Avenue South
Minneapolis, MN 55419
www.jumplibrary.com

Library of Congress Cataloging-in-Publication Data

Names: Spanier, Kristine, author.
Title: Thailand / by Kristine Spanier.
Description: Minneapolis, MN : Jump!, Inc., 2020.
Series: All around the world
Includes bibliographical references and index.
Identifiers: LCCN 2018049422 (print)
LCCN 2018050813 (ebook)
ISBN 9781641286671 (ebook)
ISBN 9781641286657 (hardcover ; alk. paper)
ISBN 9781641286664 (pbk.)
Subjects: LCSH: Thailand—Juvenile literature.
Classification: LCC DS563.5 (ebook)
LCC DS563.5 .S69 2020 (print) | DDC 959.3—dc23
LC record available at https://lccn.loc.gov/2018049422

Editor: Susanne Bushman
Designer: Leah Sanders

Photo Credits: Preto Perola/Shutterstock, cover; Littlekidmoment/Shutterstock, 1; Pixfiction/ Shutterstock, 3; imageBROKER/Superstock, 4; Balate Dorin/Shutterstock, 5; nimon/Shutterstock, 6-7; PEET Photo/Shutterstock, 8t; Ryo_stockPhoto/ iStock, 8b; Nitikorn Poonsiri/Shutterstock, 8-9t; Xiebiyun/Shutterstock, 8-9b; Travel mania/ Shutterstock, 10; William Bode/Dreamstime, 11; wararat_photos/Shutterstock, 12-13; Sean Pavone/ Alamy, 14-15; SAYAM T/Shutterstock, 16l; Ekkachai/ Shutterstock, 16r; Derek E. Rothchild/Getty, 17; Paul Kingsley/Alamy, 18-19; Xinhua/Alamy, 20-21; syolacan/iStock, 23.

Printed in the United States of America at Corporate Graphics in North Mankato, Minnesota.

TABLE OF CONTENTS

CHAPTER 1

WELCOME TO THAILAND!

Eat spicy noodles. See a buddha that stands 197 feet (60 meters) tall. Where? Roi Et. Welcome to Thailand!

buddha

There are many islands off the coast. The Phi Phi Islands have beautiful beaches! Many **tourists** visit.

Bangkok is the **capital**. The Chao Phraya River flows through it. Boats carry goods through the city. Like what? Flowers. Rice. Produce. They make floating markets!

DID YOU KNOW?

This country was once called Siam. Thailand means land of the free. Thai people have always controlled their own government.

leopard

banteng

Siamese crocodile

Asian elephants

About one-third of the country is covered in forests. Many animals live in them. Like what? Leopards. Bantengs. Siamese crocodiles. Asian elephants are here. So are tigers.

WHAT DO YOU THINK?

Forests once covered more than half of the country. What happened? Trees were cleared for farming. Others were **logged**. How can people help protect forests?

CHAPTER 2

LIFE IN THAILAND

Farmers here grow many **crops**. Rice grows on **terraces**. The cities offer many jobs. People may make computers. Clothing. Jewelry. Cars, too!

rice terrace ·····▶

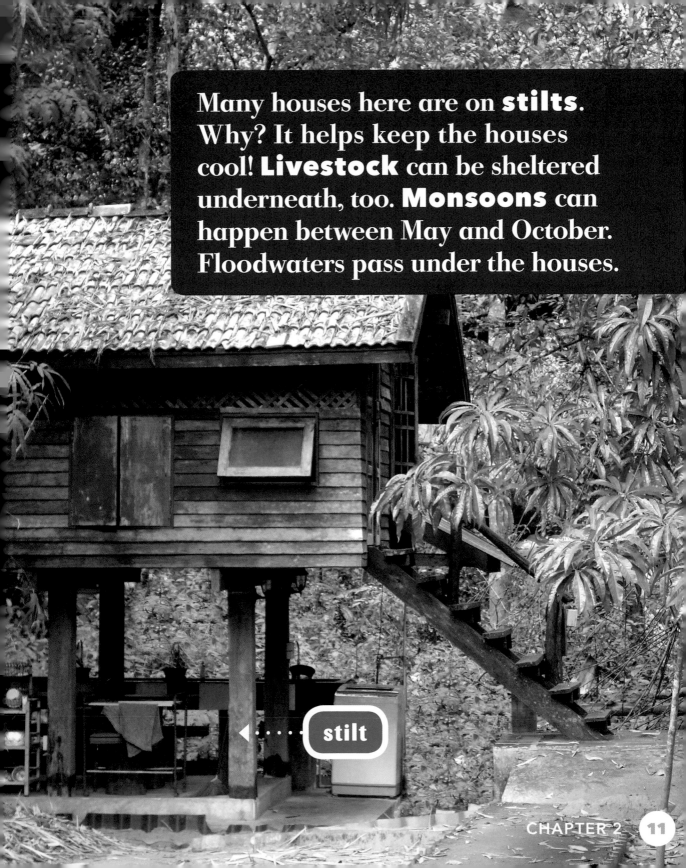

Many houses here are on **stilts**. Why? It helps keep the houses cool! **Livestock** can be sheltered underneath, too. **Monsoons** can happen between May and October. Floodwaters pass under the houses.

stilt

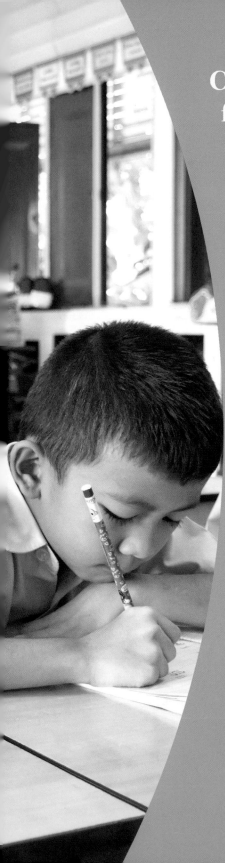

Children here go to school for at least nine years. There are strict rules about dressing. Students wear uniforms. Some schools even require students to have special haircuts!

What do students study? Math. Science. History. Buddhism. They take computer classes, too.

DID YOU KNOW?

Children bow to teachers in Thailand. To parents, too. Why? It shows respect.

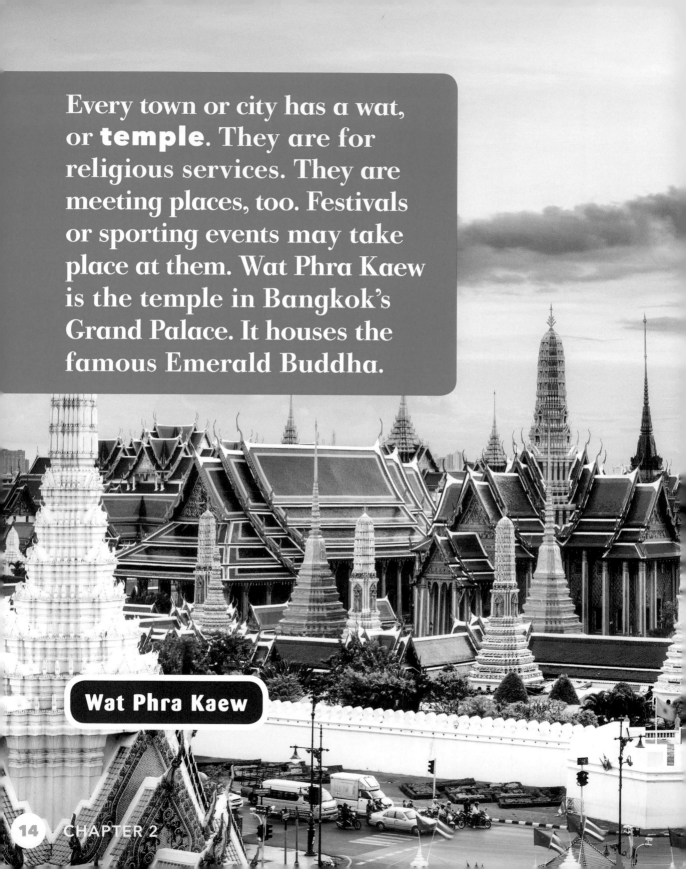

Every town or city has a wat, or **temple**. They are for religious services. They are meeting places, too. Festivals or sporting events may take place at them. Wat Phra Kaew is the temple in Bangkok's Grand Palace. It houses the famous Emerald Buddha.

Wat Phra Kaew

TAKE A LOOK!

Most people here practice Buddhism. What other religions do people follow here? Take a look!

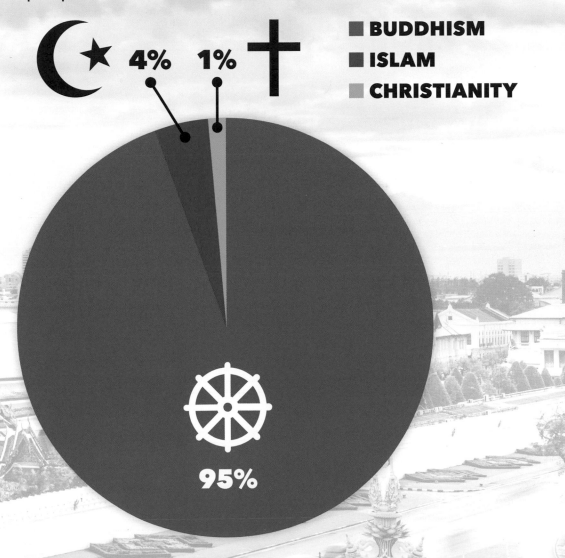

4%   1%

BUDDHISM
ISLAM
CHRISTIANITY

95%

CHAPTER 3

FOOD, FUN, AND HOLIDAYS

Food here is made with curries, chilies, and other spices. Pad thai is rice noodles stir-fried with meat and vegetables. Tom yum is a salty, spicy lemon soup.

tom yum

pad thai

satay

Satay is barbecued meat on a stick. It is served with peanut sauce. Rice is served with all meals.

sepak takraw

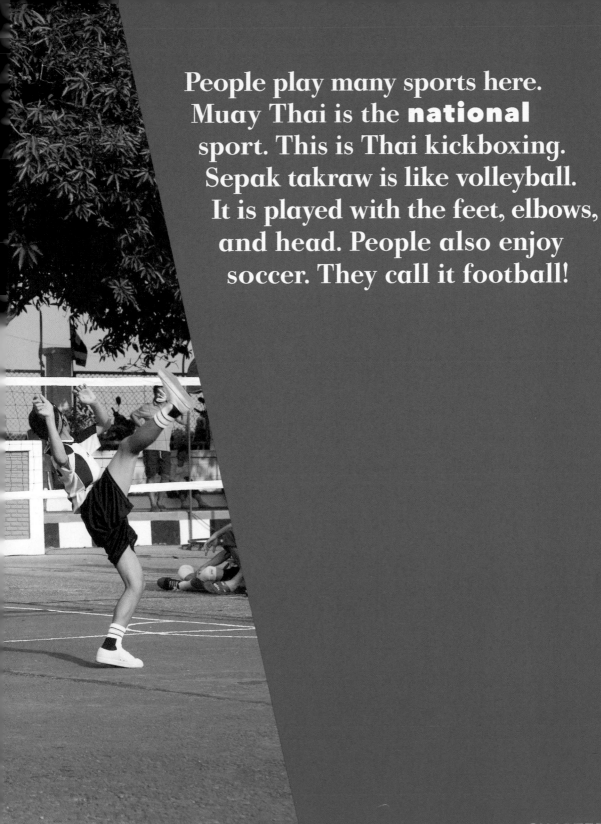

People play many sports here. Muay Thai is the **national** sport. This is Thai kickboxing. Sepak takraw is like volleyball. It is played with the feet, elbows, and head. People also enjoy soccer. They call it football!

Thai people celebrate the new year three times! International New Year. Chinese New Year. And Thai New Year. This is called Songkran. Loy Krathong is in November. People float flowers and candles in waterways. They believe they will carry their worries away.

Thailand is a land of wonder. Would you like to visit?

WHAT DO YOU THINK?

Thai people celebrate many different holidays. What holidays does your family celebrate? Which is your favorite? How do you celebrate it?

QUICK FACTS & TOOLS

AT A GLANCE

THAILAND

Location: southeastern Asia

Size: 198,117 square miles (513,120 square kilometers)

Population: 68,615,858 (July 2018 estimate)

Capital: Bangkok

Type of Government: constitutional monarchy

Languages: Thai, Burmese

Exports: automobiles, computers, jewelry, precious stones, food

Currency: baht

GLOSSARY

capital: A city where government leaders meet.

crops: Plants grown for food.

livestock: Animals that are kept or raised on a farm or ranch.

logged: Cleared and cut down for lumber.

monsoons: Seasons or storms that bring heavy rain.

national: Of, having to do with, or shared by a whole nation.

stilts: Posts that hold a structure above the ground or water level.

temple: A building used for worship.

terraces: Raised, flat platforms of land with sloping sides.

tourists: People who are traveling for pleasure.

Thailand's currency

TO LEARN MORE

Finding more information is as easy as 1, 2, 3.

1 Go to www.factsurfer.com

2 Enter "Thailand" into the search box.

3 Click the "Surf" button to see a list of websites.

FACT SURFER